BEYOND RECONCILIATION

How to Establish Long-Lasting, Life-Giving Relationships Across Racial Boundaries

Larry Jackson and Michael Fletcher

Wagner Publications

Beyond Reconciliation

ISBN 978-1-5802-018-8

Published by
Wagner Publications
11005 N. Highway 83, Colorado Springs, Colorado 80921
www.wagneipublications.org

Cover design by Tudor Maier

TABLE OF CONTENTS

INTRODUCTION

Murders in the Dark

Michael James and Jackie Burden had no idea what awaited them that cool December evening as they left the house for a late night walk. Sure, Old Wilmington Road was known as a tough street, but they felt safe. What they didn't know was that James Burmeister was out looking for an opportunity to earn a spider on his skinhead tattoo. They had no idea that Malcolm Wright, who had already obtained his spider, would be schooling young Burmeister in the art of racial execution. But Michael and Jackie soon found out. As their faces were pushed into the dirt, their hands pulled behind their backs, and the barrel of the gun pressed against their skulls, they found out. And so did the rest of the world.

Randy Meadows, the driver of the vehicle and companion to Burmeister and Wright, was quickly apprehended by the police. He panicked and told all. The next day, the whole world heard the details of the grizzly tale. National news services poured into Fayetteville, North Carolina to cover the story and wait for the real story to erupt. But nothing happened—not what they expected anyway. There was no racial uprising, no marches in the streets, no retaliatory killings. There was just peace.

A City Reacts

Nothing happened because something had already happened. Long before Meadows, Burmeister, and Wright left the bar in search of victims, something had happened, in the natural and in another realm. What most people completely missed was that these horrible murders were inspired by the rulers of darkness as retaliation for that "something" that had already occurred. There was a war going on; two powers were fighting for control of the city. This night darkness, it seemed, had triumphed.

The next day, on my way to work out, I heard the news report that two people had been killed in racially-motivated murders just two blocks from where our church had held a block party for citizens of the housing project we had adopted and only one block from the local church pastored by my new friend, Rev. Lee Downing. Lee and I had met two weeks before this tragic event and nine days prior to our block party. God knit our hearts together. In an afternoon, we had become fast friends. This would soon be tested.

Upon hearing the news I shouted, with deep anguish, “NO, NO!” The car containing the racist assassins, according to police reports, cruised through four or five predominately black neighborhoods and passed by thousands of potential victims before settling on these two from “our” neighborhood. I don’t normally talk to the devil but I did that day. I said, “Devil, you’ve messed with the wrong people and now you're going to pay!" The war had just escalated.

Pastor Downing risked his reputation and future on a newly formed cross-cultural friendship and a passion in his own heart to demonstrate reconciliation to the community in a way they could receive. Together, we put together a reconciliation rally to attempt to bring healing to the city. Having little time to plan and no opportunity to advertise, we had no idea of what to expect. But God showed up, so did the city, and so did the media. Cameras lined the walls and reporters were everywhere. The salt and pepper crowd included city, county, and military officials, in addition to business people and professionals, community residents and church members.

Gathering For Peace

Three had come into the neighborhood for hate on that horrible night, but eight hundred showed up for healing. People wept as the victims were remembered. They nodded in agreement as racism was denounced. They shuddered under the impact of identificational repentance. They literally cheered as declarations of peace and racial harmony were thundered from the pulpit. No one could have anticipated that healing moment when members of the victims' families stood and responded to the whole event with the statement, "Because of this night, we have been healed, and we forgive!" That was it! What the devil had meant for evil, God had turned to good. The light of forgiveness had dispelled the darkness of hate and a new passion for racial reconciliation had ignited in the hearts of the people.

The Place of Reconciliation

"Something" had already happened that made all this possible. Churches, led by pastors with vision, had been working months earlier, to bring the people out of the four walls of the church and into the city. God had begun to put into their hearts the need to build relationships with each other across racial and denominational lines. Who knows how many meals had been shared by pastors with leaders of other races and groups with whom they formerly had little or no contact? Who knows how many hours pastors and leaders had prayed together for revival and reconciliation? Who knows how many hours of prayer had already been logged-in as pastors stood with the Mayor in holy agreement for real and lasting change to come to the city? How many churches were adopting neighborhoods or working with the homeless? How many churches were prayerwalking in neighborhoods beyond the normal reach of the location of their building? How many pulpit exchanges had there been? How many joint services had been held across racial and denominational lines? How many people had been healed of racial wounds in the giant reconciliation event held at the civic center and broadcast over nineteen counties the year prior to these horrible murders? How many hours of service to the community had churches put in together across racial boundaries? How much damage had been done to darkness for which these killings were retaliation?

The truth of the matter is that we had already been to the place of reconciliation. Many people have been to this place They have been on their knees, confessing personal prejudice. They have been in the meetings—national and local—where they, among others, streamed to the altar, clinging to members of other races in repentance over the sins of the past. The trouble is that few know how to go beyond reconciliation to establish relationships that are redemptive in nature. The kind of relationships that make a difference; the kind of relationships that lead to lasting change. That is what this book is all about. *Beyond Reconciliation* is about a journey into a "brave new world" of living, growing, redemptive relationships that act as beacons of hope in the midst of cultures clashing in darkness.

CHAPTER ONE

The Pathway to Reconciliation

Michael Fletcher

The world is looking for racial reconciliation and can't find it. No matter what we do, it seems the goal of true reconciliation is as unattainable and unreachable as ever. Racially oriented gangs populate our streets. Militant groups on all sides of the racial question continue to propagate doctrines of hate. The President of the United States even ordered a commission to study the problem. We are facing a crisis with no apparent solution.

The Church:
A Reconciling Organism

The simple truth is that true racial reconciliation is right under the world's nose. It is in the church. By her very nature, the church is a reconciling organism. In fact, reconciliation is at the very core of the ministry of her Founder and the absolute thrust of her mission. Scripture is clear that the mission of the church is to first reconcile people to God and then to each other.

The highest priority is certainly placed on the vertical relationship. In order to go to heaven, people must be reconciled to God. But in order to live effective and wholesome lives here on earth, people must function horizontally in right relationship with each other. Doesn't John admonish us "If anyone says, 'I love God,' yet hates his brother, he is a liar. For anyone who does not love his brother, whom he has seen, cannot love God, whom he has not seen." (1 John 4:20)?

Paul encourages his readers in Philippians 2:1-11 to live lives that reflect the attitudes demonstrated by Christ:

"If you have any encouragement from being united with Christ, if any comfort from his love, if any fellowship with the Spirit, if any tenderness and compassion, then make my joy complete by being likeminded, having the same love, being one in spirit and purpose. Do nothing out of selfish ambition or vain conceit, but in humility consider others better than yourselves. Each of you should look not only to your own interests, but also to the interests of others. Your attitude should be the same as that of Christ

Jesus: Who, being in very nature God, did not consider equality with God something to be grasped, but made himself nothing, taking the very nature of a servant, being made in human likeness. And being found in appearance as a man, he humbled himself and became obedient to death—even death on a cross! Therefore God exalted him to the highest place and gave him the name that is above every name, that at the name of Jesus every knee should bow, in heaven and on earth and under the earth, and every tongue confess that Jesus Christ is Lord, to the glory of God the Father."

This passage obviously speaks to individuals, calling them to a life of humility and servanthood with a clear promise of promotion as a result. But lost in that perspective is that this passage, when viewed from the vantage point of culture, holds the key to true and lasting reconciliation. Understanding this "hidden truth" is the pathway to being enabled to live a life as an agent of true reconciliation.

A New Perspective

When I came to Christ I had to pass through the cross. There my identity was changed. I became a new creature. "Therefore, if anyone is in Christ, he is a new creation; the old has gone, the new has come!" (2 Cor. 5:17). The interesting thing is the context of this verse. First, the overall context is one of reconciliation. Second, the verse immediately prior points us to a new perspective on people.

"So from now on we regard no one from a worldly point of view. Though we once regarded Christ in this way, we do so no longer. Therefore, if anyone is in Christ, he is a new creation; the old has gone, the new has come! All this is from God, who reconciled us to himself through Christ and gave us the ministry of reconciliation: that God was reconciling the world to himself in Christ, not counting men's sins against them. And he has committed to us the message of reconciliation. We are therefore Christ's ambassadors" (2 Cor. 5:16-20).

The trouble is that when I came to Christ, I came to Him as a white, middleclass North American. While I left my sin there at the cross, I took my personal identity and its natural perspective on culture with me. And that is the rub. As a believer, I am no longer to view people from a natural perspective, from a worldly point of view. The perspective I am to have of people cannot be drawn from my culture. It must be drawn from the Kingdom. I am a new creature. Old things have passed away. *All* things have become new. I must now view people as God views people. But does that mean I ignore their culture?

Let's take another look at Philippians 2:1 - 11 passage quoted above from a cultural rather than a personal vantage point. Read it again. This time read it with the idea in mind that you are an Asian or African-American or Caucasian. Identify with the passage. Go ahead, read it again right now. Once you do, you'll realize the powerful implications here.

Christ is to be our example. He left His culture completely behind. Any personal and cultural ambition was gone.

He wasn't trying to push some agenda, trying to get ahead or make His way in this world. He wasn't trying to make it easier for "people like Himself." He laid all that down. He esteemed others more highly than Himself. He entered our culture and became like us for a redemptive purpose. He put our "culture" (humanity) above His own (divinity). Yet His "cultural" past made Him uniquely able to give to us what we desperately needed: salvation and forgiveness of sins. He didn't leave His divinity behind. He brought it with Him into our culture, giving His entrance into our culture redemptive value.

A Redemptive Purpose

The application to your life is clear. You were born into your particular race for a reason. Your race and culture has a redemptive purpose but you'll only discover it if you take the same attitude Christ had. You aren't here for yourself or even for your race. You are here for someone else and someone else's race. You are here to serve others. The needs of your race are no longer your concern. Your "agenda" is full of the needs of the races around you.

The world pushes its own agenda, which is that everyone looks out for themselves and their own people. If we live our lives this way, how are we any different than the world? What hope do we have of bringing lasting change?

If you are white, your service to those once held in slavery takes on redemptive value as, in humility, esteeming the needs of African-Americans above your own, you break down walls of hatred and mistrust. If there is injustice towards blacks in your town that is your problem. Don't let the black people carry that burden. Don't leave them to right their own "wrongs." Take that burden upon your-self. Biblically, it *is* your burden.

If you are black, let the injustice go. Don't defend yourself. That is exactly what the world does. It's natural thinking. No one experienced the level of injustice that Jesus did. Who can say they are completely innocent on all counts and, as such, totally undeserving of being wronged?

In the face of ultimate injustice, Jesus kept completely silent! Why? He wasn't here for Himself. He came for others. He left the righting of all wrongs concerning Himself to someone else—His Father. He would take no personal revenge. He simply endured the slurs and cutting remarks spawned in a misunderstanding of His culture. They even accused Him of being demonized! Yet He remained quiet.

Agents of Reconciliation

When I came to Christ, I came to the cross. When He forgave me there, I became an agent of reconciliation. My white, middle-class North American culture now has redemptive value. I have now been empowered by the cross to adopt the same attitude Christ had and lay my life down for those I formerly misunderstood. I can model the reconciliation found at the cross in my own life.

My "whiteness" means something now; something more than a natural identification of my skin color. It is my ticket to servanthood. It is my opportunity to "kill" people with kindness; my opportunity to demonstrate to people that Christ isn't like the world; my opportunity to represent the church as she has been called to be.

Why would black people who have needs of their own take up the burden of the Native-American? Only Christ! Why would white people, with financial needs of their own treat the inner city as if it were their own neighborhood? Only Christ! Why would

Native-Americans, dispossessed as they are, seek to aid in the cultural assimilation of the Hispanic migrant worker? Only Christ!

One might ask, "If I lay my life down for those I formerly misunderstood, won't I risk being misunderstood myself?" No. You won't risk being misunderstood—you *will be* misunderstood! That is all part of the redemptive process. If you are going to heal hurts in people, you are going to get hurt yourself.

First Death, Then Life

Nothing is more endearing than a person who dies well. As we watch Jesus go silently to the cross, His lips releasing forgiveness in the face of horrible injustice, our hearts break. We are drawn helplessly to Him.

What can make us act in this same way? In our case the answer is simple, "There is nothing in me that can enable me to respond this way. I am a typical middle-class white man. This response you see comes from Christ in me. That is the way He is. That is where this love I have for you comes from.

That is why I can't hate you even though you wronged me. I wronged Him and He never hated me. Instead, He forgave me. So, I forgive you." As I read it, that is the message of the cross.

You may be asking, "But if I lay my life down, won't I lose it? Who will look after me and right the wrongs done to me and my culture?" The most exciting part of the Philippians 2 passage is the part where God the Father highly exalts Jesus.

Everyone and every culture wants to be exalted but we don't necessarily want to go through the pain of qualifying. Notice the exaltation is on the other side of the cross. First the cross, then the exaltation. First death, then life. But, you can't lose your life without finding it! When you lose your life, you discover your redemptive purpose. "Whoever finds his life will lose it, and whoever loses his life for my sake will find it" (Matt. 10:39).

Stones of Servanthood and Sacrifice

People want to develop relationships with those from other races and cultures, hoping those relationships will enable them to live out a dream of living life as a “reconciled” person. The trouble comes in how those relationships are built. You can’t build lasting relationships on your own terms. The pathway to reconciliation is paved with stones of servanthood and sacrifice.

To build relationships that grow, you have to love people, not just the idea or the concept of reconciliation. The pathway to reconciliation passes through the cross. The trouble with the church today is that she, in large part, is not culturally reconciled. We have the cross in our individual lives but not in our culture. We still view people and other cultures from a worldly perspective.

In doing so, we have lost the redemptive value of our own culture and have nothing with which to build relationships that will produce reconciliation.

Right now, right where you are, go to the cross. Repent of your culture which has not been crucified. Tell the Lord you accept the responsibility of being an advocate for those from other races. Ask Him to guide you into circumstances where you can lay your life down in service for others. Repent for seeking to develop interracial relationships to benefit you. Ask Him to help you see your life as His to spend, to benefit those who are different from you.

Remember, Jesus:

1. In humility, considered us better than Himself. (Your culture is not the most important one to you anymore. The most important culture to you is the one your culture has offended.)

2. Placed our interests above His own. (Your agenda is defined by the needs and the injustices done to other cultures.

Particularly, those injustices perpetrated by your own culture.)

3. Assimilated into our culture. (You can't serve people you don't know. You don't call them to you. You go to them on their terms.)

4. Died in the process of serving us. (You embrace misunderstanding, accept suspicion, and rejoice in miscalculations of your motives.)

5. Found His redemptive purpose in serving others from a culture who had rejected His. (The highest calling in life is

serving others. Didn't Jesus wash Judas' feet?)

6. Captured our hearts and won eternal relationships with millions. (God will reward your heart with real and lasting friendships built on Christ not guilt-motivated activity.)

7. Was exalted by His Father as a result. (In the Kingdom, the way up is down!)

CHAPTER TWO

Meet Me At the Throne

Larry Jackson

I met Michael Fletcher for the very first time at 7:00 a.m. on a cool Wednesday morning in a downtown hotel in Fayetteville, North Carolina. Several times before this meeting I had thought about visiting his church during the week in order to introduce myself to him. You could almost say that there was a divine set-up that brought us together. There were some in the Fayetteville community who had confused our churches with one another because the names were so similar. Michael served as pastor at Manna Church and the name of my church was Manna Christian Fellowship.

After serving as an elder, administrator and worship leader for many years, I was sent to Fayetteville, NC, to plant a sister church by Bishop Wellington Boone who served as pastor for our church, Manna Christian Fellowship, in Richmond, VA. The fact that the names of our churches were so similar to one another was truly a coincidence. In addition to being a newcomer to the city of Fayetteville, I commuted weekly from Richmond, VA, which made it virtually impossible for me to get established in the city, let alone meet the pastor of the church whose name was so close to ours.

Divine Preparation

Before our meeting on that Wednesday morning, God prepared both of us to meet each other in different yet similar ways, without either of us being aware. The key to understanding reconciliation in general and cross-cultural friendships in particular, is that they are orchestrated by God. As His people, we need to develop the ability to discern between the divine appointments He gives us and a chance encounter, and learn how to follow through with the former.

Michael, had visited the massive revival that was taking place in Argentina, associated with Evangelists Ed Silvoso and Carlos Annacondia . There he met men and women who told him that the spirit of revival had visited Argentina as a result of brothers and sisters in Christ coming together in unity across denominational lines.

After his trip to Argentina but several months before we met, Michael and his elders also visited the Toronto blessing revival services in order to investigate the phenomenon that many people in Church were reporting as a supernatural outpouring of the spirit. Please understand, my purpose in telling this story is not to validate the revival in Argentina or Toronto; that is God's business. I am, rather, reporting how these moves of God were used to bring us together! While attending the Toronto meeting, the power of God came on Michael in his hotel room. He envisioned the Cumberland County Auditorium in Fayetteville filled with believers worshiping together. Michael returned home after each of these events determined to see revival where he lived.

In conjunction with what was happening in Michael's life, some very powerful, God-shaping occurrences were taking place in my life as well. While Michael was in Argentina, I was attending my very first Promise Keepers meeting in Dallas, Texas. Bishop Wellington Boone, who was one of the speakers for that event, told me that this was one of the greatest moves we had ever seen in our day and I needed to witness it for myself. Thousands of men filled football stadiums and basketball arenas not to cheer for a team but to worship and cheer for their God! These two-day meetings were filled with Christians and non-Christians worshiping and listening to nationally and internationally known speakers. It truly was a move of God since it was difficult to get men to attend a simple church service and actively participate.

My only hesitation in attending had to do with the work I was given to complete for our organization, and not to mention my duties as a new church to pastor. At that time another trip in addition to the trek I was making twice a week from Virginia to North Carolina wouldn't make my life any easier. However, despite my especially heavy workload, I agreed to attend the event.

Many times, our divine appointments don't come at convenient times, but when God is moving and I find out about it, my heart follows. Dr. Henry Blackaby's advice is, "Find out what God is doing and jump on board!"

A Heart for Fayetteville

While in Dallas, I expressed to Bishop Boone what Father was revealing to my heart about the city of Fayetteville. He gave me instructions to look for other pastors with the same heart or even those who would simply be willing to listen.

While in Dallas, I also met Jack Munday, who was newly hired by Promise Keepers as a staff member to serve in North Carolina. We experienced an instant connection and spent the better part of an hour discussing ways to reach the state and my views on why revival should start in Fayetteville, NC.

The Promise Keepers event was exciting and blessed but something more happened for me, God used it to deepen my resolve to see revival and to give me instructions on how to start.

I went back to Fayetteville with the zeal to see something awesome take place in our city. Not knowing about the March for Jesus meeting and prayer walk that was planned, I called for a meeting of pastors, which only a few attended. Despite the low turnout, I was not discouraged; even one willing heart would have been enough for me! On that very day, Michael was at the March for Jesus meeting talking to pastors in attendance about coming together for prayer and revival, the very thing that God placed on my heart so powerfully.

Two weeks after Michael and his elders left the Toronto Blessing, the pastors and leaders lead by Bishop Boone traveled to Toronto to experience the outpouring for ourselves. While attending the meeting, the power of God came upon me so strongly while I was in my hotel room that members of our group had to physically carry me to the evening service.

Father was showing me all of the things He was going to do in our organization and in the city of Fayetteville, from unifying the pastors to bringing revival to the city. Does this sound familiar?

Now, Michael and I had the same experience in similar ways without either of us knowing or having an opportunity to meet. The Spirit of God is a master conductor and He knows when each instrument should be played and for how long. He was conducting our lives that would later result in a great sound.

A Divine Appointment

After returning from Toronto, my new church in Fayetteville experienced a time of refreshing. Many of our members who didn't attend the revival in Toronto experienced the same touch that those who attended experienced!

It was after the culmination of these experiences and events that Michael and I met, that cool Wednesday morning in the downtown hotel banquet room provided by the owner for the purpose of prayer.

This particular gathering was a prayer meeting Michael had organized to facilitate the vision in his heart. Another pastor, Al Brice, who was also new in the city, invited me to the prayer meeting. Another important thing Bishop Boone told me and I witnessed him modeling was to never be concerned about taking the lead and getting credit. Even though a vision of revival and renewal came to me in Dallas and Toronto I didn't have to lead the effort. That attitude would have hindered God and caused me to make a different sound than the one He was producing. It is so important that Christians seek to serve first, and lead second. This goes for everything, but especially for those special things that God places on our hearts. We will always hinder His will if we insist on being in charge and doing things our way, and we will certainly never make progress in reconciliation without being willing, able, and excited to serve others.

After a focused prayer meeting the floor was opened giving us an opportunity to introduce ourselves and share our vision and experiences. When my turn came, I shared about my experience in Toronto and how our church was also experiencing the spirit of the blessing. I continued by sharing how I thought God wanted to pour out His grace and revival on our city.

During the meeting, Michael felt that the three of us, (Michael, Al Brice and myself), would work together. When the meeting was over and everyone had left, we were the only three remaining and, as some have said, "the rest is history!"

It was the beginning of a covenant friendship that has proven to transcend culture, denomination, and race.

Meeting At the Throne

Now in the eyes of most, Michael and I met that Wednesday morning. However, this is not the way it happened at all. Father is the Alpha and the Omega, the First and the Last, the Beginning and the End. This means that while He is performing something for the first time, it is also His last time. We are living in time, but living for eternity. Therefore, even though we are on the earth serving God and each other, in eternity we are also around His throne.

According to Revelation 5 and 7, people from every race and kindred who name Jesus as Lord are there. When I came to this understanding, it became apparent to me that I met Michael Fletcher at the throne of God. At the throne, everyone's attention is on the Father, in perfect unity and love. We are reconciled to our God and His Christ and through Him reconciled to each other.

Everything that is done in the earth through the lives of believers should show the world what is taking place in the heavens. Sound too spiritual? Look at what the Bible says about where we should focus our attention. "If ye then be risen with Christ, seek those things which are above, where Christ sitteth on the right hand of God. Set your affection on things above, not on things on the earth" (Col. 3:1-2, KJV).

Unless we can see the eternal purposes of God and destiny for His people, all our ministry efforts will be little more than maintaining temporary institutions with a Christian label. Michael and I met at the throne, because we were both seeking after the eternal purposes of God for our lives, our churches, and our city. Since we were both listening to Father, it was easy for Him to direct our paths, and connect us for His glory.

The Point of Reference for True Reconciliation

I have taken part in many special church or ministry services designed to instruct those in attendance about the need for and biblical precedent for reconciliation. My feet have been washed more times that I can number as a demonstration of reconciliation. This is a nice gesture but actually it doesn't prove reconciliation it is the Biblical model our Lord gave of servitude.

Please don't get me wrong, I'm aware that it takes a great deal of humility to wash feet, but in some of these meeting it was now the popular thing to do. As though this was the one act that determined reconciliation but afterwards then nothing else was done. Michael Fletcher never washed my feet nor did I wash his feet but we were absolutely reconciled and we walked it out for all to see.

The problem with reconciliation meetings, as I see it, is the point from which those who organize them started. Many start with the premise of division based on race, nationality, or cultural background, which I agree needs to be rectified, or at least addressed.

However, we have not gone back far enough if we start with skin color or geography as reference points. The qualities of race and culture, however central they may be to our identity on earth, are temporary. We have to go all the way back to the beginning for our point of reference if we hope to achieve true reconciliation in the church.

Let me explain. Would you agree that the spirit of a person has no race, sex, or earthly origin? There is neither Jew nor Greek, there is neither bond nor free, there is neither male nor female: for ye are all one in Christ Jesus. (Galatians 3:28)

Would you also agree that our bodies only house the person we are; namely, our spirit? If this is true, then look at the way our awesome Father set it up for those of us who dwell around the throne!

Our assignment is to win the lost. The lost think we are like them because we look like them, talk like them, and live with them. This plan of God to allow His people to walk the earth in the flesh was never to separate those of us who have accepted the finish works of the Lord Jesus Christ!

Modeling Heaven

I coined the term spiritual twins to represent our unity and work together not because we have the same skin color or the same earthly parents, but because we have the same eternal purpose and the same heavenly Father. Even people in the body of Christ wonder how two men of different races and backgrounds could meet late in their lives and love each other the way we do. We have a Jonathan-David relationship that has provoked other Christian leaders to love each other in the same way. Because we walk in the earth as brothers, reconciliation is not something we preach, but something we live and teach through our actions.

Our churches love and respect each other. The people at my church cannot get enough of Michael. I have seen strong evidence of great love and respect from his church for me as well. One of the doctors who works near my church regularly visit our services and participate in our special events. Many of the leaders of Michael's church has invited me to lunch and to speak for their events. Ironically, we have not held one special service for the black and white people to meet and feel good about each other. Don't misunderstand me—I don't believe that there is anything wrong with that. However, I think our success shows that there may be a better way to cause churches to get along; that is, by getting their pastors in real unity!!!

As I mentioned earlier, because of our unity, other leaders have come into divine unity as well. Whites with whites, blacks with blacks, and blacks and whites are all learning how to model heaven while their feet are still touching the earth.

The Language of Purpose

You cannot look for skin color, but rather for purpose. When you meet someone in the earth by the grace of God who speaks the same language of purpose you speak, connect with that person. By the way, men, this could be a woman or, ladies, a man. Don't put any restrictions on the Lord, but do follow common sense and scriptural guidelines when working with the opposite gender (of course that should go for anything you do).

What I have found about my relationship with those with whom I have divine and common purpose is that each of us will work very hard to protect against misconception about the relationship. We are very aware of the lines that should not be crossed, and we respect them. This means living above reproach before our families, our church members, and our communities. There are many ways that people working for the cause of reconciliation can and will be targeted by the enemy.

The enemy can attack a cross-cultural relationship in many ways, and offense is just one. The enemy may try to entice a person to get out of balance by putting ministry before family, which is always a recipe for disaster.

My friendship with Michael which began at the throne of God in the realm of eternity has provided both of us with insight, excitement, and mutual encouragement! Ultimately it is the revelation of synergy, the whole being greater than the parts put together, that is necessary for divine unity between any two people, but especially across cultures.

Michael and I understand that we didn't do God a favor by becoming friends, He did us a favor by connecting us on earth the way were in the heavenlies! We have simply embraced what He has called us to, and come into His purposes more fully, by being committed to one another.

So get before the Lord, embrace all He has for you, and let's meet at the throne!

CHAPTER THREE

The Journey Beyond: A Brave New World

Michael Fletcher and Larry Jackson

Now we come to the heart of the matter. With God using so many leaders to bring the message of reconciliation across our country, and with so many individuals coming forward at conferences to become "reconciled," why are so few people experiencing what we have experienced? Why are so few Christian individuals enjoying a real covenant relationship with a brother or sister of a different cultural background? Why are so few churches becoming truly multiethnic? And why are so few cities being impacted to the degree that the press has no race riot or protest to report after a major hate crime?

What the church must realize is that reconciliation messages and meetings, while important, are only the starting point. Just as coming forward for an altar call to receive salvation is just the beginning of a new life in Christ, so coming forward at a conference to repent of prejudice and become "reconciled" to our brothers is only the beginning.

Sanctification is both a natural out-working of legitimate salvation and a goal to be deliberately pursued, and so is walking out the lifestyle of reconciliation. It must be consciously worked towards, and yet it will not ultimately be achieved by works, but by the grace of God.

Seeing Reconciliation from God's Perspective

As we mentioned earlier, reconciliation is a message hidden throughout the Scriptures. It does not replace or displace anything else that God has specifically called us to do. When we met, it was as two pastors seeking God for the salvation of our city. We were not seeking racial reconciliation for its own sake— we were seeking revival. God revealed to both of us, as we came to His throne, that such reconciliation would be an integral part of the revival He desired to bring. Just as the ministry of reconciliation is woven into God's redemptive plan for all humanity, we found it was woven into His redemptive plan for our city. Our relationship was a result of a common purpose and united vision, not a political alliance formed for mutual benefit.

Many secular and religious organizations are trying to produce activities and programs that will address and solve the issue of race. God's vision for His people is so far beyond that. The reason the church must be reconciled is because we will be worshiping God together for eternity. The Kingdom that God wants to establish through His people on earth must reflect every aspect of that reality, or it will not accurately represent His heart.

If we think we can do the work of God without walking out the life of reconciliation in our personal relationships, we are presenting a distorted view of heaven to our children, our communities, and our nation. If we think we can successfully achieve reconciliation without the Creator of all people, we are not only deceived, we are missing the point of our existence.

Well-meaning people speak of being "color-blind" as a way of expressing that race and culture have no meaning to them, and that they are void of prejudice. Not only are these statements usually proven false under pressure, they do not reflect the heart of God. God sees our "color" or culture just as much as He sees our gender. It is a part of the identity He gave us. We did not choose it, nor are we able to.

The way to unity between Christians of different cultures is not through denying our upbringing. We come into unity by learning to appreciate and love one another for every aspect of who we are. We come into unity by learning to love the unfamiliar.

Let's look at a natural example. Every married couple has dealt with relationship challenges caused by the fundamental differences between men and women. Yet, a husband and wife don't come into unity by denying their gender, nor by trying to become the same gender. The Christian husband however, must relinquish the qualities that may be typically defined as part of his "masculinity" that are not in line with Christlikeness. Likewise, the Christian wife must die to any part of herself out of line with Jesus' character, even if she was brought up to believe it was "feminine."

That's how it is with our cultures: every culture has aspects in line with God's ways, as well as tendencies that have to be left at the cross. Actually, restricting yourself to a monocultural circle of close friends allows for a lot more hidden sin that is never dealt with! How will you ever know about areas you are not delivered in if you are only around people who deal with the same problems? That's how it is with bondages that cover entire people groups if we never form covenant relationships with those outside our culture.

We discovered another exciting aspect of God's redemptive plan while experiencing the fruit of reconciliation in our city. When racial and cultural walls are broken down between Christians in a city or community, the denominational walls will follow. Denominational barriers are, in many ways, another form of cultural barriers. They represent a different or preferred way of understanding and doing things. Once the spirit of reconciliation touches people's hearts to the point where they will go outside their cultural comfort zones, it is often only a couple more steps in the same direction to venture outside their denominations.

Leadership for Real Reconciliation

While we would never attribute the success we have experienced on the front of racial reconciliation to anything but the grace of God, there were conscious decisions we both made as pastors and leaders that greatly contributed to this success. Those decisions have not only enabled us as individuals to experience the reality of the kingdom of God at a level we had never imagined, but they have also caused the blessings to overflow into our congregations and communities. Those decisions were prompted by the Spirit of God and will be crucial to your heavenly success as well.

In the first place, we never tried to use reconciliation as a platform to build our individual ministries. There are a lot of speakers out there with a message of reconciliation that are not necessarily walking it out in their lives. While God may anoint such a message, He desires us to go far beyond catching a revelation, to changing our lives and the lives of those around us. Seeing racial walls torn down became a burning passion in our hearts, not a catchy topic to draw speaking engagements or sell books. Because of this, we never had to strive for opportunities to get our message out; God opened every door. As a pastor or lay leader in the ministry of reconciliation, you must ask yourself, "Is reconciliation my passion, or just my platform?"

Secondly, once we had formed a covenant relationship, we refused to try to accomplish the vision alone. Once we declared that God had brought us together for purpose, we followed through by sticking together in everything. If one of us would get an invitation to minister, we would insist the other be invited as well. This was not a legalistic arrangement, but rather a revelation of real corporate purpose. The devil could have sent us our separate ways if we had allowed selfish ambition to creep into the picture, but we understood we were greater together than we were apart.

Sadly, most pastors and Christian leaders in our nation today have no idea what it is like to use their grace or favor to promote someone else with no ulterior motives. We selfishly assume that everyone else is there to help us, not the other way around. Only when we can put relationships and the higher purposes of God ahead of our personal goals, even if those goals are from God, will we experience true reconciliation and unity. Only then will our congregations and ministries see an example they can follow with success.

Lastly, but perhaps most important, we were determined to move beyond meetings and programs and into real relationship. Our homes were open to one another, not just for strategy meetings, but for Sunday dinners and regular fellowship time. We know one another's families, and our wives share the same closeness we do.

As we mentioned earlier, our congregations know and love each other, without ever having had a "formal" joint service. When real relationships are established, programs become an afterthought. The breakthroughs then happen at the altars of one another's homes, over coffee, or watching our children play together, not necessarily while holding hands during a conference or special service.

Many Christians make the mistake of assuming that once they get excited about being unified with brothers and sisters of other cultures that they have automatically "arrived" at the place of walking in that unity. This often leads to presumptuous attitudes, and later disappointment. Just because you are excited about being reconciled to your black brother doesn't mean you understand what it is like to be black. Just because you are eager to become close to your white sister, doesn't mean you know what she needs to hear to feel comfortable with you. Just because you are the leader of a congregation of thousands who love you doesn't mean you have earned the trust and respect of the Asian-American pastor down the street. Such things come by relationship, not programs. Those who are truly walking in reconciliation, and leading others in the same direction, are in it for the long haul.

Practical Steps to Walking in Reconciliation

Here are five basic steps that we believe all Christians who are serious about walking in reconciliation should take to see that it happens in their lives:

1. Invite your friend(s) from another culture into your inner circle. Everyone has different "circles" of relationships, from our closest friends and relatives to our most casual acquaintances. Most so-called reconciliation stops at the outermost circle. We love to claim that "black friend" or "Hispanic brother," but how often do they drop by your house just to hang out? Do you know their children, their parents, or where they grew up? As Christians, we should be known as individuals whose innermost circle of friends consists of all kinds of people, not just those culturally similar to ourselves.

You may discover while trying to become closer to someone of another culture that some of your close friends or family do not share your enthusiasm. In fact they find your new friendships uncomfortable or unnecessary. Many feel that "getting along" is good enough and there is no need to intermingle, but remember that the same arguments were made in favor of continuing segregation. Don't give up, but don't allow others' prejudice to harm your friends either. Seek to protect them as you would like to be protected in their position.

2. Seek to enter the inner circle of your friend(s) of different culture. It is not enough to invite others to be with you in your cultural comfort zone. You must desire to be with them, in their church or their normal environment, and honor them above yourself. At the same time, you must be invited in, and not try to enter presumptuously. Are you willing to go somewhere that does not feel natural to you? Are you willing to feel uncomfortable? Are you willing to become accustomed to a new set of norms? Unless you are, you will never walk in the fullness of what God has intended for your relationships.

We have found that most pastors who claim to desire a "multicultural" church really want people of different cultures to come and conform to their established way of doing things. That is not reconciliation anymore than an empire that politically "unites" several different countries for the gain of its emperor! God is not calling you to accumulate friends of different cultures as different colored feathers in your cap. He is calling you to change and grow and learn from all the people He places in your life. People are not projects, and as long you treat them that way, you will miss the point of what God is trying to do in you and through you.

3. Prepare for internal conflict and conviction. During the American Civil War, it was often said that it was easy for whites in the north to champion the cause of abolition from a distance, since they were never around black people themselves. It is always easy to tout rhetoric and hot air about reconciliation as long as you never have to confront your own inner prejudice. Walking in real relationship with members of another culture will enhance or bring out any unresolved issues or offenses you may not even realize you carry. Your theology may be ruffled. Your feelings may be hurt. You may be shocked or offended at the way others think or express themselves.

Prepare yourself, because your flesh will not die without a fight. It will be extremely easy to say to yourself that you gave it your best shot, or that this must just not be the person God is calling you to. It will be very easy to speak to someone who will sympathize with you about your offense, rather than confessing it to the Lord and going to your brother or sister as the Bible says to do. The devil always makes it easy to give up, but if you take his invitation, you will never change.

4. Become a student of culture. Christians should not be culturally ignorant people. If we serve the Creator of all people, how can we be narrow-minded and underexposed? With the exception of those raised in a bicultural or multicultural family, most of us have been members of one culture for our whole lives. We become experts on how to relate to those like us, but are completely clueless about others. Become a student of other cultures, and learn to fall in love with what you are studying. Remember, as a student, you are trying to learn about how to function in another culture, not trying to fIx it, or change it into what you think it should be.

Think about yourself. What kinds of food does your family eat? What music do you listen to? What kinds of movies do you watch? What kinds of books do you read? What color are the people in the picture books you read to your children? What kind of art hangs on your walls at home? Take opportunities to learn about other cultures from your friends, as well as from books, movies, music, and travel. Be a good example for your children, and educate them about such things at home, so that when they are your age they will be ahead of the game.

5. Seek opportunities to demonstrate reconciliation. We all know that faith without works is dead, and we should all get excited about chances to demonstrate that we are different than the world. Most often these opportunities will come in the form of being misunderstood or mistreated. Don't see this as something unusual or out of the will of God, but take the opportunity to demonstrate a Christlike response. Most American Christians today are so hedonistic that they think any kind of pain is the devil attacking them, when it is really God setting them up with an opportunity to be like Jesus.

Remember that no one is perfect, and the new friends God is placing in your life are no exception. Remember that you are not perfect either, and extend the same level of grace and mercy to others that you would want for yourself. These are elementary biblical principles that really apply to all relationships, but are so often overlooked. Being determined to walk in reconciliation will prevent you from skipping these required courses, and move you not only toward being more culturally educated, but being more like Jesus.

Is there any hope for reconciliation in America? Yes. The hope is hidden in the church. Is there hope for the American church? Yes. We believe we are living proof that there is hope. Our prayer is that Holy Spirit would convict each one of us as to where we have been walking below the Father's standard for our lives and relationships, and that each of us would cooperate with His efforts to change us and our world!

www.ingramcontent.com/pod-product-compliance
Lightning Source LLC
LaVergne TN
LVHW010544100826
845148LV00013B/2601
9781585020188